The Best Book of

Big Cats

Christiane Gunzi

KINGFISHER

NEW YORK

Contents

4 Meet the big cat

6 A world of big cats

Created for Kingfisher by
Picthall & Gunzi Limited

Author and editor: Christiane Gunzi
Designer: Floyd Sayers
Editorial assistance: Lauren Robertson
  and Jill Somerscales
Natural history consultant: Julie Childs
Illustrators: Martin Knowldon and
  Mick Loates

KINGFISHER
Larousse Kingfisher Chambers Inc.
95 Madison Avenue
New York, New York 10016

First published in 2001
10 9 8 7 6 5 4 3 2 1

1TR/1100/WKT/MAR/128KMA

14 The first big cats

16 Lion king

LIBRARY OF CONGRESS CATALOGING-IN-PUBLICATION DATA
Gunzi, Christiane.
  The best book of big cats / by Christiane Gunzi.
    p. cm.
  ISBN 0-7534-5337-1
    1. Panthera—Juvenile literature. [1. Panthera.
    2. Cats.]

QL737.C23 G86 2001
599.75'—dc21
            00-049724

Printed in Hong Kong

24 Champion racer

26 Cat cousins

8 Growing up

10 Perfect hunters

12 Cat talk

18 Cool cat

20 Spotted killer

22 Secretive cat

28 Big cats in danger

30 Studying big cats

31 Glossary
32 Index

Meet the big cat

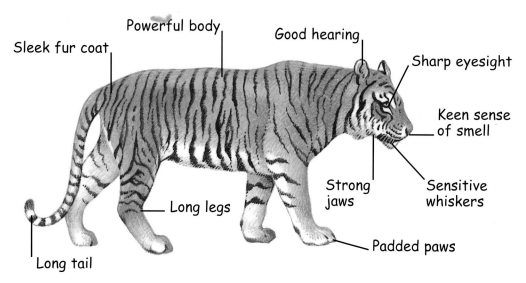

Big cats such as tigers, lions, and leopards are powerful meat-eaters or carnivores. Their strong claws and sharp teeth help them to hunt other animals to eat. Big cats have excellent hearing and sight, sleek, muscular bodies and beautiful fur coats. Today many big cats are endangered because people kill them for their fur. The most endangered big cat is the tiger.

Sleek fur coat

Powerful body

Good hearing

Sharp eyesight

Keen sense of smell

Sensitive whiskers

Strong jaws

Long legs

Padded paws

Long tail

A big cat's body

The cat's muscular body and long legs allow it to leap, pounce, and climb, and its long, flexible tail helps it to balance. On the underside of each foot are pads that act as cushions when the cat lands on hard ground. A big cat's large eyes can see well in the dark, and its funnel-shaped ears can turn to catch the smallest sound. Long, sensitive whiskers on its face help the cat to feel its way.

Siberian tiger

This is the largest, most powerful cat in the world, and only about 200 are left in the wild. The Siberian tiger's long, thick fur keeps it warm in the cold forests of China, Siberia, and Korea where it lives. In winter, its coat becomes paler in color, so pigs, deer, and other prey cannot see it as easily.

5

A world of big cats

Big cats have lived on Earth for about 34 million years, and they all belong to the same family. They are found on every continent except Australia and Antarctica. Big cats include lions, tigers, jaguars, and leopards. The cheetah is a close relative, but it is different from other cats because it has narrow paws and blunt claws, like a dog. Apart from the cheetah, jaguar, and clouded leopard, all these cats can roar. The lion's roar is the loudest.

Well disguised

Big cats are famous for their magnificent coats. Cats in hot countries have shorter fur than those in cold countries. The colors and markings on a cat help it blend in with its habitat. This disguise is called camouflage. Lions have sand-colored coats to camouflage them in dry savanna areas, and tigers have stripes to camouflage them in forests.

Clouded leopard
(Asia)
weighs 50 lb.
up to 4 ft. long

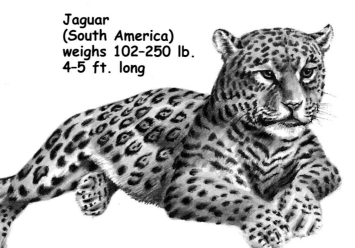

Jaguar
(South America)
weighs 102-250 lb.
4-5 ft. long

6

Snow leopard
(Asia)
weighs 55–166 lb.
4–5 ft. long

Lion
(Africa)
weighs 277–398 lb.
up to 6 ½ ft. long

Tiger
(Asia)
weighs 398–546 lb.
9–10 ft. long

Cheetah
(Africa)
weighs 99–133 lb.
4–5 ft. long

Leopard
(Africa and Asia)
weighs 144–177 lb.
3–4 ½ ft. long

7

Growing up

Baby big cats are called cubs. They grow inside their mother's body for about three months, then she gives birth to them in a safe place, such as a den or a cave. The cubs are born covered with fur, but they cannot see well or walk properly for a few days. Young cats stay with their mother until they are old enough to hunt for themselves.

Baby tigers

1 A tigress has between two and four cubs in a litter. They feed on her milk for six to eight weeks. Then she will bring them prey to eat.

2 A tiger cub learns to hunt by playing. After a few months, its mother will take it on hunting trips when it will learn to catch prey.

3 At 11 months, a tiger cub can catch birds by itself. At 16 months, it is big enough to hunt larger prey, such as deer.

Cat courtship

Big cats that are friends often greet each other with a head rub. Male and female tigers breed once a year, usually in spring. After mating, the male leaves the female. When the cubs are born, the female cares for them on her own.

A good mother

Every few days, the female leopard carries her cubs to a new hiding place so that jackals, hyenas, and wild dogs cannot find them. Sometimes she has to leave the cubs hidden for several days while she goes in search of food.

9

Perfect hunters

Lions, tigers, and other big cats are expert hunters. They have powerful legs for chasing, and strong jaws and sharp teeth for biting. Big cats eat all kinds of animals—gazelles, wild pigs, rabbits, and fish. Usually hunting at dawn or dusk, they silently creep up on their prey. They pounce quickly and grab the animal by the neck or throat.

Catching prey

Lions are the only big cats that hunt animals larger than themselves. Lionesses often hunt in groups. They chase antelopes, zebras, gazelles, and wildebeest. Although the lionesses do the hunting, the lions always eat first.

Lionesses chasing a young oryx

Pouncing tiger

Tigers usually hunt alone at night, and often close to water. Before they pounce on prey, such as muntjac deer, they have to get close to them, because tigers can only run in short bursts.

Cat talk

Big cats make all kinds of sounds to communicate with each other. They purr, growl, hiss, and roar. One big cat will signal to another by twitching its tail and moving its ears. An angry cat will growl and flick its tail to warn another cat not to come into its territory. If rival cats get into a quarrel, the smaller, weaker animal usually gives in to the larger, stronger one before a fight can begin.

Roaring

A lion roars to talk to other members of his pride. This is the loudest sound made by any cat, and it travels a long way.

Making faces

People can tell a lot about big cats by watching their eyes and ears. If a cat is happy and content, it sits with its eyes half-closed. If it is frightened or surprised, its eyes are big and round. Ears flat on the head mean that the cat is annoyed or afraid. When a cat is really angry, it holds its ears close to its head, opens its mouth wide, and shows its long canine teeth as a warning to other animals.

Content (eyes half-closed)

Alert (ears pricked)

Frightened (eyes wide open)

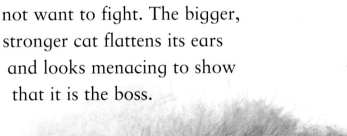

Angry (ears flattened)

Who's boss?

When one cat is afraid of another cat, it lies down to show that it does not want to fight. The bigger, stronger cat flattens its ears and looks menacing to show that it is the boss.

Smilodons

These saber-toothed cats lived in family groups in North and South America. They killed mammoths and other large mammals with their long, sharp teeth. The last *Smilodons* died out about 8,000 years ago.

14

The first big cats

More than 20 million years ago the first relatives of today's big cats lived on Earth. They are known as the saber-toothed cats and they looked a bit like lions and leopards. Saber-toothed cats were carnivores with massive canine teeth for killing and eating their prey. The saber-toothed cat that we know most about is *Smilodon*. It was slightly larger than today's lion and very fierce.

Saber-toothed cat

Lion

Open wide

The saber-toothed cat could open its mouth very wide. It had such long teeth that when it closed its mouth, they stayed on the outside.

A modern-day lion has smaller canine teeth than its ancient relatives. It does not need such large teeth because it kills prey by suffocation, not by biting it.

15

Lion king

Lions are the largest, most powerful cats in Africa. A few lions are also found in India. Lions live in family groups, called prides, and there can be up to 30 lions in one pride. The male lion is the only big cat with a mane around his head and chest. This thick fur makes him look larger than he really is and helps him frighten away enemies. The mane also protects a lion during a fight.

Family pride

The male lion does not help the female lionesses to raise cubs. His job is to protect the pride against intruders. If a rival tries to enter his territory, he roars loudly. If two lions fight, the winner becomes king of the pride. The loser has to leave and find somewhere else to live.

Scratching post

A lion scratches trees to mark his territory. He leaves claw marks and a strong smell to show others that this is his home. The next time the lion passes by, he sniffs the spot to check that his scent is still there.

Catnap

A pride of lions spends much of its time relaxing and sleeping. Lions only hunt when they are hungry, and the males leave the hunting to the females. Sometimes lions eat the remains of food left by hyenas and other scavengers.

Lions use their teeth and claws when they fight over territory.

Cool cat

The tiger is one of the most magnificent creatures on Earth. This powerful predator lives deep in the forest, where it stalks deer and wild pigs in the long grass. It spends much of its time hunting and must eat about 100 large prey a year. Tigers need a huge area to hunt in, and their territory can be as large as 62 square miles. Apart from the jaguar, the tiger is the only big cat that enjoys water.

White tiger

Tigers with pale fur are called white tigers. They are very rare. White tigers have brown stripes instead of black stripes, and their eyes are blue instead of yellow.

Tiger types

Scientists believe that there are only about 5,000 tigers living in the wild. The five types that survive today are the Siberian, Bengal, Caspian, Sumatran, and Indo-Chinese tigers. These cats are found in Asia, and all are in danger of extinction.

The Caspian tiger has the longest fur

The Sumatran tiger has the closest stripes

The Siberian tiger has the palest fur

The Bengal tiger has the shortest fur

The Indo-Chinese tiger has the darkest fur

Storing food

When a tiger catches a deer or other big animal, it usually drags it to a quiet place. This can sometimes be over half a mile away. When the tiger has eaten enough, it covers the dead animal with leaves and grass so that other creatures cannot smell it. The tiger may return later to finish its meal.

Tiger lazing in a forest stream to keep cool

19

Leopard's lunch

Leopards eat all kinds of animals, including big and small birds, small and medium-sized mammals, and even insects. After eating, leopards like to drink at a water hole.

Cricket

Aardvark

Rabbit

Hornbill

Ostrich

Baboon

A heavy meal

A leopard's prey can weigh as much as the leopard itself. It is hard work for the cat to carry its meal up into a tree. The leopard uses the branches of the tree for storing and protecting its food to eat later.

Spotted killer

The leopard is good at climbing and often carries its prey into the branches of trees to keep it safe from hyenas, jackals, and other scavengers. Leopards live alone most of the time, and they can survive in all kinds of habitats, including the forests of Asia and the African savanna. A leopard's eyesight and hearing are six times better than a human's. This helps leopards escape from poachers, who want to kill them for their beautiful coats.

Leopard dragging a dead gazelle into a tree

Black magic

A panther is, in fact, a black leopard. If you look closely at its coat, you can just see its leopard spots. Black panthers live like other leopards. They are found in the forests of Asia and some areas in Africa, and they are becoming very rare.

Cloudy coat

The clouded leopard lives in the forests of India, Nepal, and southeast Asia, and is hardly ever seen. Its teeth look more like a saber-toothed cat's than any other cat's teeth. Unlike other leopards, it does not roar.

Secretive cat

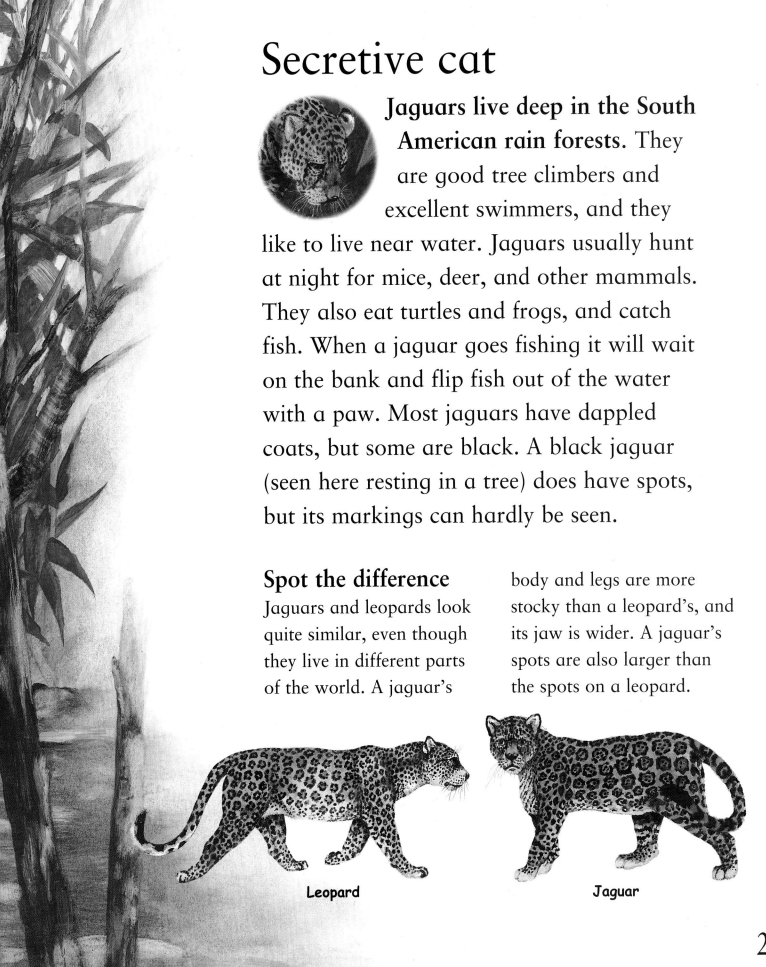

Jaguars live deep in the South American rain forests. They are good tree climbers and excellent swimmers, and they like to live near water. Jaguars usually hunt at night for mice, deer, and other mammals. They also eat turtles and frogs, and catch fish. When a jaguar goes fishing it will wait on the bank and flip fish out of the water with a paw. Most jaguars have dappled coats, but some are black. A black jaguar (seen here resting in a tree) does have spots, but its markings can hardly be seen.

Spot the difference

Jaguars and leopards look quite similar, even though they live in different parts of the world. A jaguar's body and legs are more stocky than a leopard's, and its jaw is wider. A jaguar's spots are also larger than the spots on a leopard.

Leopard

Jaguar

Champion racer

The cheetah is the fastest mammal on Earth. With its slim body and long legs, it is the perfect shape for running and leaping. The cheetah lives on the African savanna. While lions and leopards are sleeping during the day, the cheetah hunts for antelopes, gazelles, hares, and rodents. Male cheetahs usually live in groups of four or five, and they guard their territory fiercely. Females usually live alone, except when they are looking after a litter of cubs.

From a standstill, a cheetah can reach top speed in three seconds.

Hiding in the grass

To keep newborn cheetah cubs safe from leopards, hyenas, and other predators, their mother carries them to a new hiding place every few days. The cubs usually live with their mother for up to 20 months. They have long, grayish fur on their backs. This may help disguise them when they hide in long grass.

Fast as the wind

In short bursts, a cheetah
can chase prey at speeds of
up to 62 miles per hour—
more than twice as fast as
the best human sprinters.

Run for your life

Gazelles flee when they see
a cheetah. The cheetah chases
them, but if it does not catch
one after a minute or so, it has
to stop because it gets tired.

25

Cat cousins

The big cats also have many smaller relatives. The puma, lynx, serval, ocelot, and caracal are all wild cats. These cats are related to the domestic cats that people have at home. Most of the smaller wild cats live in wooded areas, on high mountains, or even in hot deserts. They cannot roar like the big cats, and their young are called kittens instead of cubs. Smaller wild cats hunt rats, mice, rabbits, birds, and insects, just like domestic cats.

Puma
(North and
South America)
weighs 80-228 lb.
3-7 ft. long

Cat acrobats

All these wild cats are quick and agile, and they climb and jump well. They usually hunt animals smaller than themselves and can leap high into the air to catch birds and insects as they fly past.

Siberian Lynx
(Asia)
weighs 18-62 lb.
2-4 ft. long

Ocelo
(North and
South America)
weighs 24-33 lb.
2-3 ft. long

26

African wildcat
(Africa)
weighs 7–18 lb.
20–29 in. long

Caracal
(Africa and India)
weighs 13–42 lb.
2–3 ft. long

Serval
(Africa)
weighs 20–40 lb.
2–3 ft. long

Tiger in the house

Domestic cats learn how to survive by
playing, just like big cats do. When
you see a kitten pouncing on
a ball of wool, it is easy
to imagine its cousins
hunting in the wild.

Lynx
(North America)
weighs 11–38 lb.
2 1/2 –3 ft. long

Big cats in danger

Every year, huge areas of land are cleared to make space for houses, roads, and farms. Forests, grasslands, and other habitats are destroyed. These areas are home to big cats and many other animals. When animals lose their homes, it is difficult for them to find food and shelter. If we do not protect the places where big cats and other wild animals live, one day they will only live in zoos and wildlife refuges.

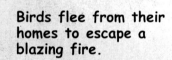

Birds flee from their homes to escape a blazing fire.

Burning bright

When a grassland or a forest is burned to clear land, the animals and plants that live there are in danger, and many are killed. These areas are the habitat of tigers, leopards, and other rare mammals.

Poaching

People have been hunting big cats for their fur for thousands of years. Today, it is illegal to kill wild cats, but a few people still hunt them. The animal's fur, bones, teeth, and meat are sold. It is difficult to protect big cats in the wild from poachers. The cats roam over huge areas, and there are not enough people to guard them.

Guards arrest a poacher in Africa.

The skins of leopards and other big cats have been made into fur coats.

Why big cats are killed

In some parts of the world, cats are killed to make fur coats, and their bones are used in medicines. This is not necessary because coats can be made from fake fur, and ingredients other than big cat bones can be used in medicine.

Powdered tiger bones have been used in medicine because some people believe they have special powers.

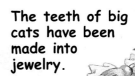

The teeth of big cats have been made into jewelry.

Studying big cats

It is important to protect big cats in the wild so we can save them from extinction. Experts watch cats in their natural habitat to find the best way to look after them. They may put a collar with a radio transmitter around a cat's neck. The transmitter sends out signals that help the experts follow the cat and discover where it likes to live in the wild.

A group of lionesses in a safari park

Tracking big cats

The Snow leopard is found only in the high mountains of Asia, so it is difficult to track down unless it has a radio collar on. Radio collars help scientists find and take care of these beautiful cats in the wild.

Seeing big cats up close

You can see big cats at a safari park or in a wildlife refuge, where they have room to roam around. Visitors can drive along and watch the cats from the safety of a car or jeep. It is not safe to get out of the car when you are around big cats.

Glossary

camouflage The different colors and markings on an animal that help it hide in the wild.

canine teeth The long, pointed teeth that cats have for eating meat.

carnivores Animals, such as cats, that eat meat.

carrion An animal that has been killed, but is not yet completely eaten. Animals, called scavengers, will eat the remains.

communicate This is how all animals "talk" to each other. It may be by smell, by voice, or by the way that the animals stand or move.

domestic cat A small cat that lives with people.

endangered An animal or plant that is in danger of dying out forever. Many big cats are endangered.

extinct An animal or plant that has died out forever is extinct. Saber-toothed cats are extinct.

habitat An animal's habitat is its natural home in the wild. A cheetah's natural habitat is the African savanna.

illegal There are laws to protect all of us, including big cats. Something that is against the law is illegal. It is illegal to kill big cats.

mammals Animals, such as cats, that are covered with fur or hair, give birth to live young, and feed them milk.

mane The long, thick fur on a lion's head and shoulders. The lion is the only big cat that has a mane. It makes him look bigger than he really is.

poachers People who hunt and kill wild animals, such as big cats, are called poachers. It is against the law to poach big cats.

predators Animals that hunt and prey on other animals. Cats are predators.

prey These are animals that are hunted and eaten by cats and other predators.

pride This is the name for a family group of lions. Lions are the only big cats that live in family groups.

rodents Small mammals, such as rats, mice, and squirrels are rodents. They are prey for big cats.

savanna Huge, flat areas of grassland in Africa, with only a few trees.

scavengers These are animals that search for food left by other animals. Hyenas, jackals, and vultures are scavengers.

stalk To stalk is to follow an animal quietly. Tigers stalk their prey.

territory The area where an animal lives. Big cats have large territories.

Index

A
ancient big cats 14–15

B
body language 12, 13
body shape 4, 23, 24

C
carnivores 4, 31
cheetah 7, 24–25
claws 4, 6, 16–17
climbing 4, 20–21, 23, 26
communication 12–13, 31
cubs 8–9, 24–25

D
domestic cat 26, 27, 31

E
ears 12–13
endangered cats 4, 18, 31
expressions 12, 13
eyes 4, 8, 18, 21

F
fighting 12, 16–17
food 8, 10, 17, 19, 20–21
forest fires 28
fur 4, 5, 6, 18, 29

G
gazelles 10, 20–21, 24–25

H
hearing 4, 21
hunting 8, 10–11, 18, 23, 24–25, 26

I
Indo-Chinese tiger 18

J
jaguar 6, 23
jaw 4, 10, 23

L
leaping 4, 24, 26
legs 4, 10, 23, 24
leopard 6–7, 9, 20–21, 23
lion 6–7, 12, 15, 16–17
lionesses 10–11, 16, 17
lynx 26–27

M
mammoths 14–15
mane 16, 31
mating 9

O
ocelot 26
oryx 10–11

P
panther 21
paws 4, 6, 23
poaching 4, 29, 31
pouncing 4, 11, 27
prey 10, 11, 18, 20–21, 24–25, 31
pride 16, 31
puma 26

R
rain forests 18, 23, 28
roaring 6, 12
running 10–11, 24–25

S
safari park 30
savanna 21, 24
Siberian lynx 26–27
Siberian tiger 5, 18
Smilodons 14–15
snow leopard 6–7, 30
speed 24–25
swimming 23

T
tail 4, 12
teeth 14–15, 17, 29, 31
territory 12, 16, 18, 24, 31
tiger 4–5, 7, 8–9, 11, 18–19

W
water 11, 18, 23
white tigers 18
wildlife reserves 28, 30

Z
zoos 28, 30

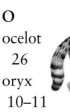